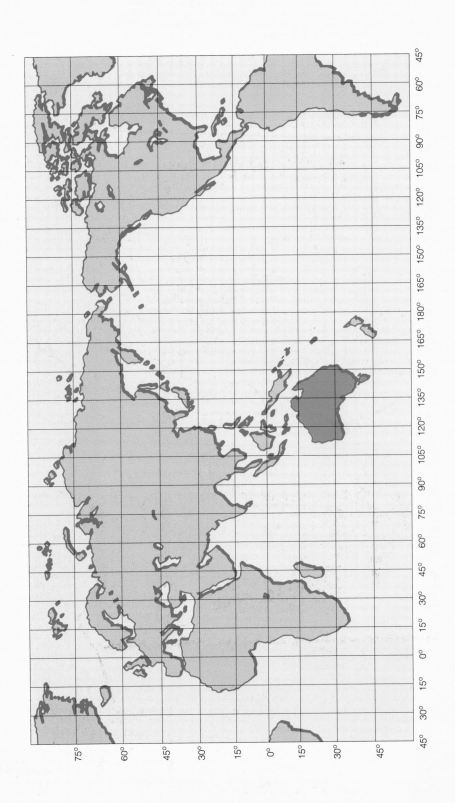

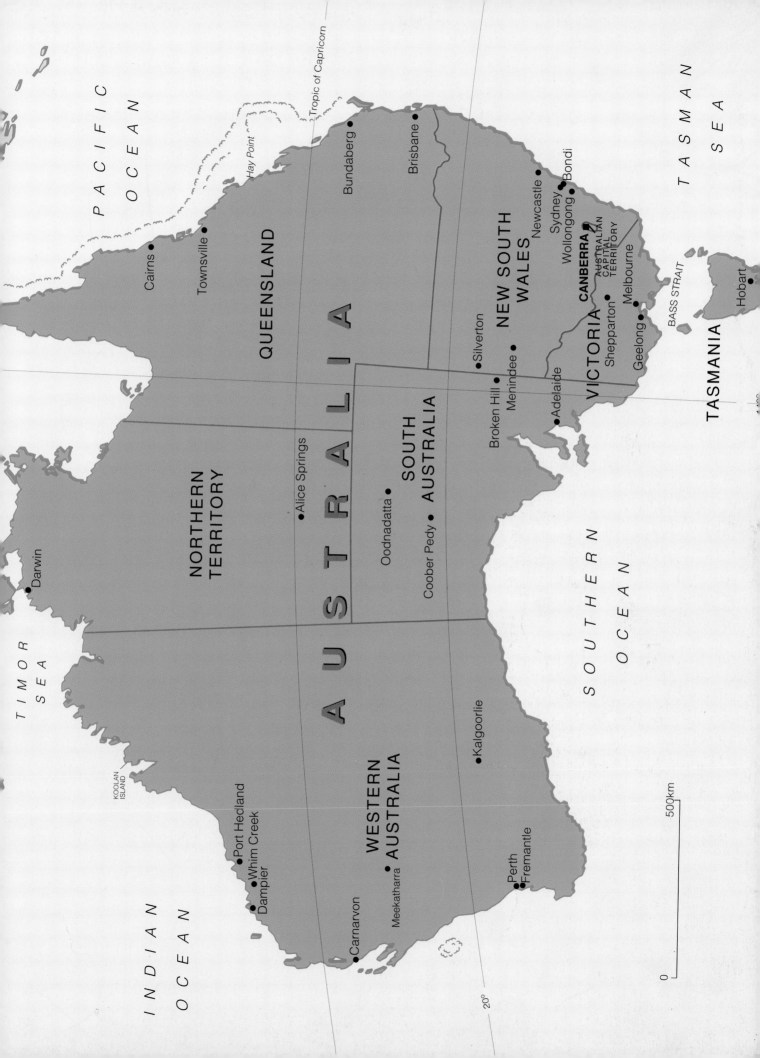

COUNTRY FACT FILES

AUSTRALIA

Robert J Allison

MACDONALD YOUNG BOOKS

First published in 1995 by Macdonald Young Books
and reprinted in 1997

© Macdonald Young Books 1995

First published in paperback in Great Britain in 1999
by Macdonald Young Books

Find Macdonald Young Books on the internet at http://www.myb.co.uk

Macdonald Young Books, an imprint of Wayland publishers Ltd
61 Western Road
Hove
East Sussex
BN3 1JD

Design	Roger Kohn
Editor	Diana Russell
DTP editor	Helen Swansbourne
Picture research	Valerie Mulcahy
Illustration	Malcolm Porter
	János Márffy
Consultant	Dr Philip Hirsch
Commissioning editor	Debbie Fox

We are grateful to the following for permission
to reproduce photographs:
Front Cover: Joanne Fox above, Zefa below;
Allsport (UK) Ltd, page 24 above right (Bob Martin); Colorific!,
pages 35 and 40 above (Bill Bachman); Robert Harding Picture
Library, pages 38/39; The Image Bank, page 24 above left
(Don & Liysa King); Mitsubishi Motors Australia Ltd, page 32;
Spectrum Colour Library, pages11 above, 17 right and 18/19
below (Diana Calder),18/19 above (G Adsett), 33, 39 and 41
(D & J Heaton), 40 below; Tony Stone images, pages 11 below
(Chesley), 20 (Fritz Prenzel), 36 below (B Chittock); Sygma,
pages 17 left (J Guichard), 29 below (Rick Smolan); TRIP/Eye
Ubiquitous, pages 27 and 42 above (Matthew McKee),
29 above (J Winkley), 43 (Sportshoot); TRIP, page 37
(T Knight); TRIP/Robin Smith, pages 8 above, 12,14,15,16,
21, 22 below 23, 24, below, 26, 28 left and right, 30, 31, 34,
36 above, 42 below; Zefa, pages 8/9, 10, 22 above (Boiselle),
25 (Damm).

The statistics given in this book are the most up to date
available at the time of going to press

Printed in Hong Kong by
Wing King Tong

A CIP catalogue record for this book is available from the British Library

ISBN: 0 7500 2807 6

Special thanks to the children of Meekathara High School, Meekathara,
Western Australia, who are pictured on the front cover.

CONTENTS

Words that are explained in the glossary are printed in
SMALL CAPITALS the first time they are mentioned in the text.

INTRODUCTION

Australia lies between latitudes 10°S and 44°S and longitudes 112°E and 154°E. It is a vast country, stretching some 3,680 kilometres from north to south and 4,000 kilometres from east to west.

The original inhabitants of Australia were the Aborigines, a dark-skinned people whose life-style is closely linked with the land and natural environment. They were the sole inhabitants of the island continent until 1788, when a boat from England arrived at what is now Sydney Harbour. The boat was full of convicts and many of the first white settlers were prisoners who had been banished from Britain and sent to the "other side of the world" for the rest of their lives. Gradually, people started to emigrate to Australia of their own free choice, and today the country is inhabited

▲*An Aborigine in a cave at Uluru (Ayers Rock), a traditional sacred site of Australia's original inhabitants.*

▼*Sydney Harbour, with the Opera House and Harbour Bridge, is one of Australia's best-known landmarks.*

by people who were originally of many nationalities — not just from Europe but from countries around the world.

Today Australia has a developed economy. Agriculture is important. There is a great range of farms, from small, specialist vineyards producing famous Australian wines, to massive ranches where cattle and sheep are reared. Industry is varied, but is particularly focused on primary production — mining raw materials, for example.

Due to its size and location, Australia has one of the most diverse range of environments on Earth, including deserts, tropical rainforests and snow-capped mountains. There are other important variations within the country, too — such as where people live, the distribution of large cities and how easy it is to get around by public transport.

AUSTRALIA AT A GLANCE

● Area: 7,686,850 square kilometres
● Population (1993 estimate): 17,827,204
● Population density: 2.3 people per sq km
● Capital: Canberra, population 310,000 (1990)
● Other main cities: Sydney 3.6 million; Melbourne 3.1 million; Brisbane 1.3 million; Perth 1.2 million; Adelaide 1.05 million
● Highest mountain: Mount Kosciusko, 2,228 metres
● Longest river: Darling, 2,739 kilometres
● Language: English
● Major religion: Christianity
● Life expectancy: 73.3 years for men; 79.9 for women
● Currency: Australian dollar, written as $A ($A 1 = 100 cents)
● Economy: CAPITALIST economy, based on agriculture and minerals
● Major resources: A wide range of minerals, including bauxite, coal, iron ore, copper, tin, silver and uranium
● Major exports: Meat, wool, wheat, machinery and transport equipment, alumina, gold, coal
● Environmental problems: Destruction of good-quality soil (for example, through poor agricultural management), SALINIZATION, DESERTIFICATION, CYCLONES along the northern coast, fresh water availability, droughts, bush fires

THE LANDSCAPE

Australia has three main landscape sub-divisions: the Western Plateau; the Interior Lowlands or Central Plains; and the Eastern Highlands, or Great Dividing Range.

The Western Plateau covers about half the continent and is flat, barren land extending more than 1,800 km from west to east. Most of it is desert. Not all the deserts have sand dunes. Some have gently undulating surfaces strewn with rocks and boulders. In the south is the Nullabor Plain, a flat, barren, limestone lowland riddled by underground caves. Much of the Western Plateau is termed the OUTBACK because of its remoteness.

KEY FACTS

● Australia covers 5.2% of the land surface of the world.
● Australia is the smallest continent and the sixth largest country.
● It is slightly smaller than the USA, half the size of Europe and less than one-fifth the size of Asia.
● Desert and semi-desert cover about two-thirds of the country.
● Australia has 25,760 km of coastline.

⑩

▲ **Uluru (Ayers Rock) in Northern Territory, one of the oldest rocks on Earth.**

GREAT BARRIER

ARNHEM LAND

GULF OF CARPENTARIA

CAPE YORK PENINSULA

KIMBERLEY PLATEAU

BARKLY TABLELAND

GREAT SANDY DESERT

HAMERSLEY RANGE

MACDONNEL RANGES

GREAT ARTESIAN BASIN

GREAT DIVIDING RANGE

GIBSON DESERT

Uluru 867 m
MUSGRAVE RANGES

SIMPSON DESERT

GREY RANGE

DARLING DOWNS

GREAT VICTORIA DESERT

Lake Eyre

FLINDERS RANGE

River Darling

NEW ENGLAND RANGE

River Swan

NULLABOR PLAIN

GREAT AUSTRALIAN BIGHT

0   500km

River Murray

AUSTRALIAN ALPS

Mt Hotham△ △Mt Kosciusko 2228 m

SNOWY MOUNTAINS

N

Mt Ossa 1617 m

LAND USE (%)
Arable land
Meadows and pastures
58
6
22
14
Other (includes built-up areas)
Forest and woodland

T-shirt, slop on some sun lotion and slap on a hat".

In the far south, Australia has what is called a temperate climate, with conditions similar to those in parts of Western Europe. In the island state of Tasmania, for example, summers are mild but in winter temperatures often drop below freezing and snow can fall.

One other interesting variation occurs along the eastern edge of the country, due to a chain of mountains. The altitude of the Snowy Mountains, Australian Alps and South-Eastern Highlands means there is more regular rainfall and snow. This is because moist air blows in from the Tasman Sea and is forced up over the mountains. As the moist air rises, it cools. The water vapour in the air condenses to form clouds and rain falls.

NATURAL RESOURCES

Australia produces 80 commercially significant minerals, including bauxite, coal, iron ore, uranium, natural gas and petroleum. Some of the reserves are massive. For instance, the Mount Goldsworthy iron ore mine in Western Australia is estimated to contain over 15,000 million tonnes. In New South Wales the silver, lead and zinc deposits of the Broken Hill mining province have already yielded over 147 million tonnes of ore. New mineral deposits are still being found, such as the copper deposit at Roxby Downs.

The economy of many towns in the outback is based on the mining industry. For example, Kalgoorlie in Western Australia developed because of gold mining, and Coober Pedy in South Australia as a result of mining opals.

Australia has large energy resources too. Some 70% of the country's petroleum requirement is met from national reserves,

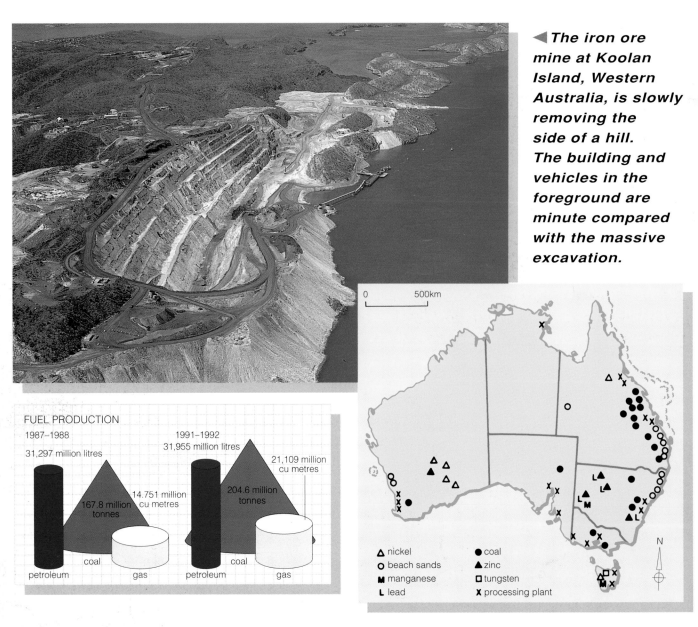

◀ **The iron ore mine at Koolan Island, Western Australia, is slowly removing the side of a hill. The building and vehicles in the foreground are minute compared with the massive excavation.**

FUEL PRODUCTION

1987–1988
31,297 million litres

1991–1992
31,955 million litres

167.8 million tonnes
14.751 million cu metres
204.6 million tonnes
21,109 million cu metres

petroleum   coal   gas   petroleum   coal   gas

0   500km

△ nickel   ● coal
O beach sands   ▲ zinc
M manganese   □ tungsten
L lead   X processing plant

while coal, which is important in generating electricity, is produced in several Australian states.

Forestry products form another key resource. In Tasmania, areas of woodland provide several timber products, including wood chips from native eucalypt forest, which are exported.

Because much of Australia is very dry, there are some major water management schemes. Some relate to the GROUND WATER

reserves of the Great Artesian Basin in the south-east. Others involve the collection and storage of water in the Eastern Highlands. The Snowy Mountains scheme in the Eastern Alps has 16 major dams, 7 power stations and many kilometres of tunnels and aqueducts. The project took 23 years to complete and cost $A 800 million. It opened in 1972.

▲ **Opal mining activities at Coober Pedy, South Australia, have produced piles of waste that look like the craters of a "moonscape".**

▶ **Windmills are used to pump water from large natural underground reservoirs.**

LEADING PRODUCERS OF GOLD AND SILVER, 1992 (tonnes)

GOLD
South Africa 608.5
Australia 240
USA 296

SILVER
Mexico 2,325
USA 1,741
Peru 1,595.2
Australia 1,248

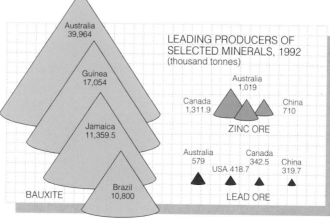

BAUXITE
Australia 39,964
Guinea 17,054
Jamaica 11,359.5
Brazil 10,800

LEADING PRODUCERS OF SELECTED MINERALS, 1992 (thousand tonnes)

ZINC ORE
Australia 1,019
Canada 1,311.9
China 710

LEAD ORE
Australia 579
USA 418.7
Canada 342.5
China 319.7

POPULATION

More than 85% of Australia's people live in towns and cities. About two-thirds live in either Sydney, Melbourne, Brisbane, Adelaide or Perth – each of which have over 1 million inhabitants. Most of the large cities are in the eastern part of the country, in New South Wales, Victoria and Queensland. Perth is the one exception, located on the west coast of Western Australia. Many people also live close to the coast. There is an almost total absence of people in the centre of Australia and large areas of land are completely uninhabited.

The white population is mostly of European origin. Over 70% have European ancestors and nearly 40% have relatives in the United Kingdom or Ireland. There is a high proportion of young people compared with other countries, partly due to the high birth rate after the Second World War and partly due to the high number of immigrants. Over 70% of Australians are

▶ *Flinders Street Station in Melbourne, Victoria, at the heart of one of Australia's largest cities. Trams or street-cars are a popular means of public transport in the city.*

▼ *A lone homestead at Silverton in the New South Wales outback. Much of the interior is sparsely populated, and neighbours can live many kilometres away.*

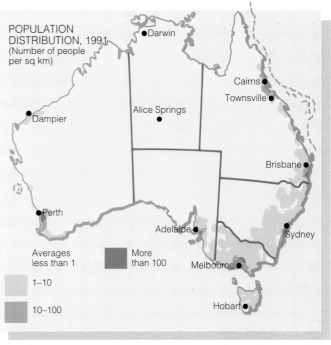

POPULATION
DISTRIBUTION, 1991
(Number of people
per sq km)

Darwin

Cairns
Townsville

Dampier

Alice Springs

Brisbane

Perth

Adelaide

Sydney

Melbourne

Averages
less than 1

More
than 100

1–10

10–100

Hobart

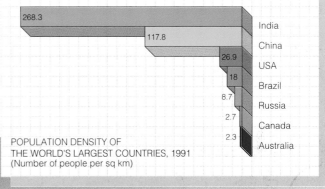

268.3	India
117.8	China
26.9	USA
18	Brazil
8.7	Russia
2.7	Canada
2.3	Australia

POPULATION DENSITY OF
THE WORLD'S LARGEST COUNTRIES, 1991
(Number of people per sq km)

◀ *An Aboriginal corroboree. The long piece of carved wood is a* DIDJERIDU, *an Aboriginal musical instrument.*

▼ *Recent immigrants have arrived from a wide range of countries. Like other Australians, most live in towns or cities.*

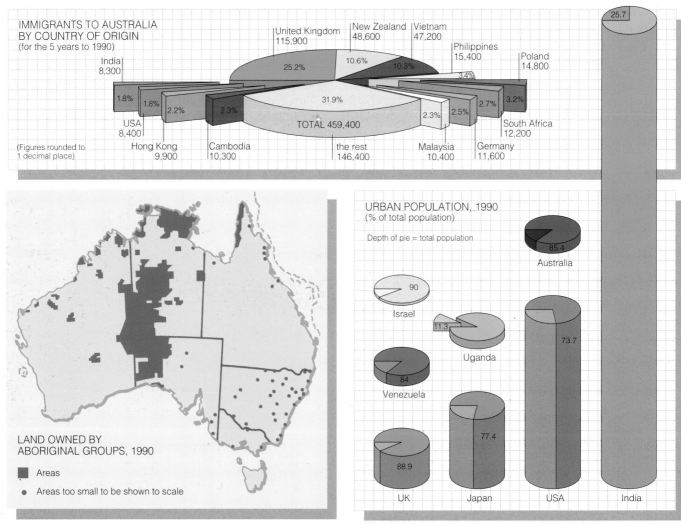

IMMIGRANTS TO AUSTRALIA BY COUNTRY OF ORIGIN
(for the 5 years to 1990)

United Kingdom 115,900 — 25.2%
New Zealand 48,600 — 10.6%
Vietnam 47,200 — 10.3%
Philippines 15,400 — 3.4%
Poland 14,800 — 3.2%
South Africa 12,200 — 2.7%
Germany 11,600 — 2.5%
Malaysia 10,400 — 2.3%
the rest 146,400 — 31.9%
Cambodia 10,300 — 2.3%
Hong Kong 9,900 — 2.2%
USA 8,400 — 1.8%
India 8,300 — 1.8%
TOTAL 459,400

(Figures rounded to 1 decimal place)

LAND OWNED BY ABORIGINAL GROUPS, 1990
■ Areas
• Areas too small to be shown to scale

URBAN POPULATION, 1990
(% of total population)
Depth of pie = total population

Australia 85.4
Israel 90
Uganda 11.3
Venezuela 84
UK 88.9
Japan 77.4
USA 73.7
India 25.7

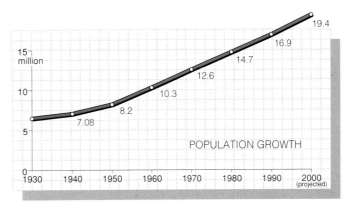

POPULATION GROWTH

less than 45 years of age (1993 estimate) and almost a quarter are under 14 years old.

The pattern of immigration has changed in recent years. After the Second World War, greater numbers of immigrants arrived from southern European countries such as Greece and Italy. Today a significant proportion of all new arrivals in Australia are from Asian countries such as Malaysia, Hong Kong, Brunei and Singapore. Recent immigrants have included refugees from Vietnam, Laos and Cambodia. Asian immigrants tend to cluster together in large cities. Many have brought important skills in industry and business which have helped the Australian economy.

The original inhabitants of Australia are the Aborigines. Although they were originally rural, nomadic people, today more than 60% live in urban areas. They form only about 1.5% of the country's population, compared with a white population of about 95% and an Asian total of 4%. Aborigines have a strong culture and sense of identity and pride. An

important idea is "Dreamtime", which represents the Aboriginal cultural, historical and ancestral heritage. They believe that Dreamtime was the dawn of all creation when the land, the rivers, rain, wind and all living things were generated. It is also the Aboriginal way of linking the past, present and future. Large groups of Aborigines meet periodically to hold a "corroboree", a ceremony where songs and dances are used in celebrations. During these gatherings, the men decorate their bodies with white paint made from soil and crushed rocks.

KEY FACTS

● There are 122.6 people per sq km in the Australian Capital Territory, compared with only 0.1 in Northern Territory.
● Each day in Australia approximately 700 babies are born and 360 people die.
● Today there are about 238,600 Aborigines in Australia, compared with an estimated 750,000 when Europeans arrived in 1788.
● Between June 1991 and June 1992, a total of 107,390 people arrived in Australia to settle permanently.

▲ *The Vietnamese community in Cabramatta, Sydney, developed as a result of immigration from South-East Asia.*

RELIGION

More than 84% of Australians belong to a religious denomination. The majority are Christian, either Protestant or Roman Catholic, reflecting the early settlers who arrived from Europe in the late 18th and 19th centuries. With the increasing number of immigrants from South-East Asia, other religions, such as Islam and Buddhism, are now growing rapidly.

EDUCATION

Literacy rates are generally high, although the Aborigines have suffered disadvantages and many cannot read or write. The school year runs from February to mid-December and education is free up to university level. Children start primary school at the age of 5 or 6 and leave at 12. Secondary education is compulsory up to the age of 15 (16 in Tasmania). School students work towards important examinations which are taken at 15 and 17 years of age. Those taken at the age of 17 are known as the Higher School Certificate, which students must pass if they

▲*Farmers in the outback often use motor-bikes rather than horses to cover the large distances between their herds of livestock.*

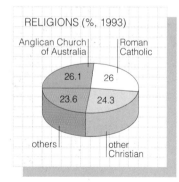

RELIGIONS (%, 1993)

Anglican Church of Australia | Roman Catholic

26.1 | 26

23.6 | 24.3

others | other Christian

▲*Most Australians are Christians, although other religions are growing.*

want to go to university.

Unique to Australia are Schools of the Air, designed to reach children who live in remote areas. Children talk to teachers during lessons using two-way radios. The first such school was set up in Alice Springs in 1951.

HEALTH

Australia's health system, known as Medicare, is open to everyone and guarantees medical and eye care. A famous part of the medical service is the Royal Flying Doctor Service, established in 1927, which allows doctors to fly in small planes to visit patients. The planes are also used as air ambulances. The RFDS operates a radio service so that people in remote areas can seek medical advice and find out what to do if someone is ill or injured.

SPORT AND LEISURE

Sport is an every day part of Australian life. Famous teams include the Wallabies, the national rugby union squad. Australia is also

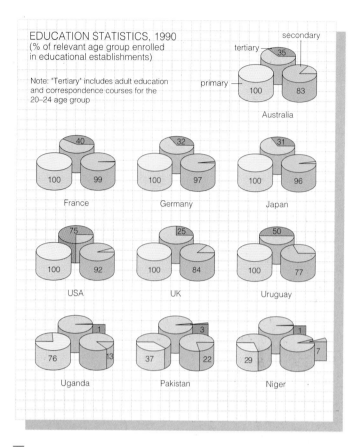

EDUCATION STATISTICS, 1990
(% of relevant age group enrolled in educational establishments)

Note: "Tertiary" includes adult education and correspondence courses for the 20–24 age group

These children in Western Australia are members of the School of the Air. They work at home and talk to their teacher over a two-way radio.

Many people in Coober Pedy, South Australia, live in caves hewn out of rock. The underground homes provide excellent shelter from the high temperatures and burning sun.

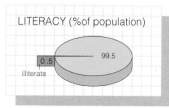

LITERACY (%of population)

◀ *Surfing is a popular sport.*

▼ *Australian Rules Football was developed in Melbourne in the mid-19th century. A match is divided into 4 quarters of 25 minutes.*

FESTIVALS AND HOLIDAYS

January 1	New Year's Day
January 26	Australia Day (celebrates the founding of the colony of New South Wales on 26 January 1788)
March or April	Easter
April 25	Anzac Day (commemorates the landing of Australian and New Zealand forces at Gallipoli in 1915 in the First World War)
Early June	The Queen's Birthday
Early October	Labour Day
December 25	Christmas Day
December 26	Boxing Day

▶ *Spare-time activities often include water sports such as water-skiing and windsurfing. These boats in Sydney Harbour are participating in the Tall Ships Race, held as part of Australia's Bicentenary celebrations in 1988.*

well known for its cricket and its Australian Rules Football. This is a mixture of Gaelic football, soccer and rugby, played with an oval ball, on an oval field, with 18 players per team. Play consists of mostly kicking or punching the ball. The Grand Final of the Australian Rules Football season is every bit as important in Australia as the FA Cup Final is in Britain or the final of the Superbowl in the USA.

Many sports are associated with Australians' love for the beach and sea. There are frequent surf carnivals in the summer at places like Bondi Beach near Sydney. Yacht teams compete for the Davis Cup, which is awarded to the winning crew of the Sydney to Hobart yacht race. Other activities include swimming, shooting, horse racing, canoeing, skiing, camping and bush-walking. Occasionally Australians will "go bush", meaning to get away from the stress of urban living for a while by trekking in the outback.

KEY FACTS

● In 1991, a total of 3,075,137 children were enrolled in primary and secondary schools.
● The average distance between classmates in the Carnarvon School of the Air, Western Australia, is 42 km.
● In 1986 there were 1,072 hospitals in Australia and 1 doctor for every 552 people (compared with 1 for every 650 people in the UK and 1 for every 419 in the USA).
● The average life expectancy of Aborigines is 15–20 years less than the national average .
● The standard working week is 38 hours long.
● The average Australian household contains 2.9 people.

▶ *These Aborigines are painting motifs using natural products. The designs are often handed down from generation to generation and form part of Aboriginal culture. Many of the shapes have important meanings related to traditional life-styles.*

◼ RULE AND LAW

Australia has a Federal Parliament with representatives from the six states, two territories and a number of dependent areas such as Christmas Island. Its system is similar to that in the United Kingdom, although members of both Houses of Parliament are elected. There are 147 seats in the House of Representatives and 76 in the Senate. Elections are held every three years. The head of the political party which wins the most seats becomes Prime Minister. In a similar manner to Great Britain, Queen Elizabeth II is head of state. She is represented in Australia by the Governor-General.

The federal government, based in Canberra, occupies the Australian Capital Territory (ACT). It is responsible for matters such as defence, foreign policy, national economic policy and immigration.

Each state and territory has its own

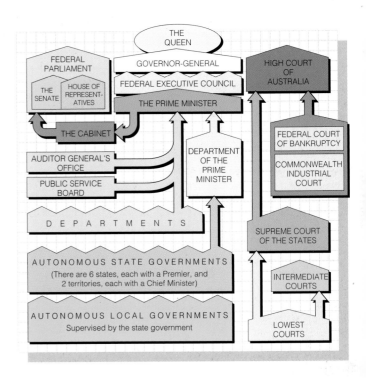

▼ *An Anzac Day ceremony in Canberra, Australia's capital city. Federal government buildings can be seen in the distance.*

- After Europeans arrived in 1788, Australia was governed from Great Britain.
- Transportation of convicts ended in 1868.
- Australia achieved independence on 1 January 1901.
- Voting is compulsory at the age of 18. People who do not vote can be fined.
- In ACT about 60% of the work force is employed by the government.
- There is one police officer in Australia for approximately every 550 people.
- Some government areas are very large – Northern Territory is 2.5 times the size of France and 6 times the size of Britain.
- As at June 1993, there were 63,200 personnel in Australia's armed forces – 28,600 in the army, 19,300 in the air force and 15,300 in the navy.

▲ *Protests about the rights of Aboriginal people, or "Kooris", have been a feature of recent years.*

government and legal systems. The head of government in a state is called the Premier and in a territory the Chief Minister. State government responsibilities include education, housing, health, the welfare of Aborigines, tourism and natural resources.

Law enforcement is divided between federal and state governments. The Australian Federal Police deals with matters like drugs, government crime and terrorism. Each state also has its own police force which is responsible for law enforcement at the local level.

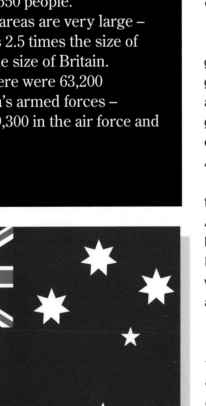

◀ *The 7-pointed Commonwealth star on the Australian flag represents the country's states and territories. The other stars represent the Southern Cross constellation.*

FOOD AND FARMING

Because of Australia's diverse climate and soil conditions, there is a vast range of crops in the country. Cereals are grown over wide areas in all states and territories, while other crops are confined to specific locations. Chief items are wheat, barley, sugar-cane and fruit such as paw-paws, mangoes, currants, grapes, strawberries, oranges and apples. Industrial crops include cotton, flax and peanuts. Wine is produced in vineyards, especially in the Hunter Valley and Barossa Valley.

The main wheat-growing areas extend in a belt west of the Great Dividing Range from New South Wales into Victoria and across the southern part of South Australia. There is

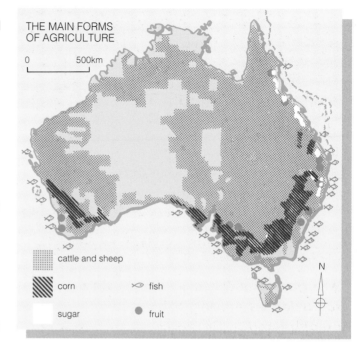

THE MAIN FORMS OF AGRICULTURE

0   500km

- cattle and sheep
- corn
- sugar
- fish
- fruit

N

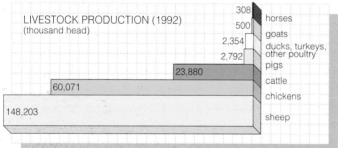

LIVESTOCK PRODUCTION (1992)
(thousand head)

Head	Livestock
308	horses
500	goats
2,354	ducks, turkeys, other poultry
2,792	pigs
23,880	cattle
60,071	chickens
148,203	sheep

▼ **There are more sheep in Australia than in any other country in the world, and the majority are in the south-east of the country. They are reared for both wool and meat.**

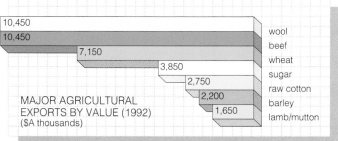

▲ *Sugar-cane farms in Australia are regarded as among the most mechanized in the world.*

10,450	wool
10,450	beef
7,150	wheat
3,850	sugar
2,750	raw cotton
2,200	barley
1,650	lamb/mutton

MAJOR AGRICULTURAL
EXPORTS BY VALUE (1992)
($A thousands)

KEY FACTS

● Only 2% of the land available for crops in Australia is cultivated.

● Although two-thirds of Australia is used for livestock farming, much of the land is dry and of poor quality.

● There are around 180,000 farms in Australia, covering a total of 482.5 million hectares.

● Australia produces about 30% of the world's total wool supply.

● Australia is the world's 9th largest exporter of wheat.

● Australia is the world's 6th largest beef- and veal-producing nation, and the largest exporter.

● Of all the mutton exported from Australia, almost 61% goes to Saudi Arabia and Kuwait.

● The Merino sheep breed was first introduced to Australia in 1797.

● The most important state for sheep-rearing is New South Wales.

● Almost 25% of Australia's cattle are dairy breeds.

● About half of the country's cattle are reared in the state of Victoria.

● The average consumption of beer per person in 1986 was 140 litres per year, compared with 73.9 litres of soft drinks, 13.5 litres of tea and 17.6 litres of wine.

◄ *Cowboys, or "stockmen", look after the cattle and maintain the fences on cattle stations.*

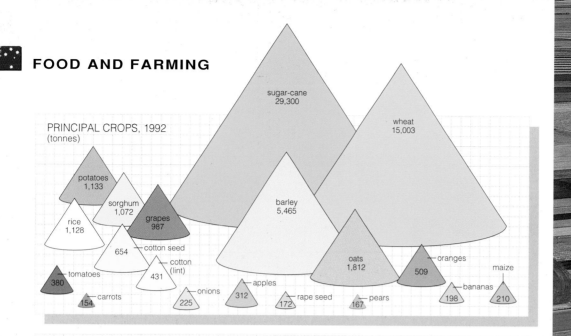

PRINCIPAL CROPS, 1992
(tonnes)

sugar-cane
29,300

wheat
15,003

potatoes
1,133

sorghum
1,072

grapes
987

rice
1,128

654

cotton seed

cotton
(lint)
431

barley
5,465

tomatoes
380

carrots
154

onions
225

apples
312

rape seed
172

oats
1,812

pears
167

oranges
509

bananas
198

maize
210

DAILY FOOD SUPPLY, 1990 (calories/grams of protein per inhabitant)

	CALORIES		PROTEIN (g)
Australia	3,385		101
USA	3,680		111
UK	3,282		94
Japan	2,926		96
Mozambique	1,803		30
Afghanistan	1,710		48

▼ *An Aboriginal child in Northern Territory about to eat a wichety grub. Other traditional foods include daisy yams and turtle eggs.*

▶ *The green rolling fields of the Darling Downs in Queensland. This is one of Australia's most agriculturally productive areas.*

also an extensive area in south-west Western Australia. Wheat yields fluctuate greatly from year to year because of erratic rainfall. The main barley-growing areas are in South Australia, while oats are grown in the south where rainfall is fairly uniform. Almost 95% of Australia's rice production is concentrated in New South Wales and 95% of sugar-cane production is in Queensland because of the warm, tropical climate. Many farms are highly mechanized.

The principal livestock are cattle, sheep and poultry. Some cattle and sheep farms

cover thousands of square kilometres in the outback. They are called "stations". Dairying flourishes in the eastern and south-eastern coastal areas and inland on the Darling Downs of Queensland. Beef cattle are more widespread. About 75% of Australia's wool production is from the Merino sheep breed.

Mullett, tuna and snoek are all caught in near-shore coastal waters. Grayling, prawns, oysters and scallops are also fished, largely for sale in Japan and the USA.

Traditionally, Australians' main meal includes meat, vegetables and a dessert,

which might be a PAVLOVA, regarded as a national dish, or a Lamington – a sponge cake covered with chocolate and coconut. Kangaroo and crocodile meat are served in many restaurants. Today there is also a wealth of foreign cuisine, partly because of immigrants arriving from Asian countries. Cantonese, Japanese, Indonesian, Thai, Vietnamese and Korean foods are all popular.

The Aborigines traditionally eat from the land. Although their diet today is very Westernized, many still know which berries are juicy and which plants are edible.

Industry employs about 30% of the Australian work force. Due to the abundance of natural resources, the country is a major exporter of agricultural products, minerals and fossil fuels, including coal, oil and natural gas.

MANUFACTURING

The manufacturing industry has been expanding rapidly, particularly since the end of the Second World War. In 1989–90 the country had 41,797 registered companies, employing a total of over 1 million people. Manufacturing is concentrated around the east coast, with the main centres in Sydney, Adelaide, Melbourne and Brisbane. Important industries are ship-building, car construction, metals, textiles, clothing, food-processing and wine.

Some cities are especially important for certain products. For example, Sydney is

▲ **Assembling Mitsubishi cars at the Tonsley Park Manufacturing Centre in Adelaide. At this point on the assembly line, the car engine is being matched to the bodywork.**

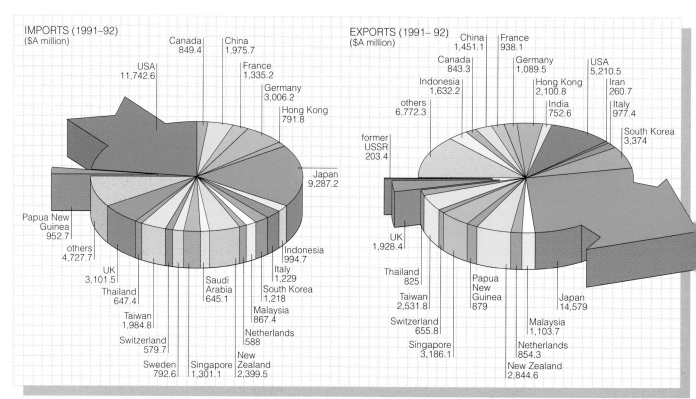

IMPORTS (1991–92) ($A million)

Canada 849.4
China 1,975.7
USA 11,742.6
France 1,335.2
Germany 3,006.2
Hong Kong 791.8
Japan 9,287.2
Papua New Guinea 952.7
others 4,727.7
Indonesia 994.7
UK 3,101.5
Italy 1,229
Thailand 647.4
Saudi Arabia 645.1
South Korea 1,218
Taiwan 1,984.8
Malaysia 867.4
Switzerland 579.7
Netherlands 588
Sweden 792.6
Singapore 1,301.1
New Zealand 2,399.5

EXPORTS (1991–92) ($A million)

China 1,451.1
France 938.1
Canada 843.3
Germany 1,089.5
USA 5,210.5
Indonesia 1,632.2
Hong Kong 2,100.8
Iran 260.7
others 6,772.3
India 752.6
Italy 977.4
former USSR 203.4
South Korea 3,374
UK 1,928.4
Thailand 825
Papua New Guinea 879
Japan 14,579
Taiwan 2,531.8
Switzerland 655.8
Malaysia 1,103.7
Singapore 3,186.1
Netherlands 854.3
New Zealand 2,844.6

noted for the production of transport
equipment; Hobart for textiles, clothing
and footwear; Shepparton for food,
beverages and tobacco. Australia's
manufacturing output is weak compared
with many other developed countries,
because many industries developed late
compared with other nations.

OVERSEAS TRADE

Australia has a relatively small domestic
market, in part due to its low population,
so trade with other countries is important.
The cost of shipping manufactured goods
abroad over large distances means that
transport expenses are high. Principal

exports include coal, gold, meat, wool,
alumina, wheat and machinery. Of
Australia's top 25 exports, 21 are raw
materials – known as primary products.
Chief imports include computer and office
machinery, transport equipment, crude oil
and petroleum products.

In the past, trade with foreign countries
was focused on countries in the West,
such as the USA and Europe, because of
historical links. Today, however, trade
with countries in the Pacific region is
increasingly important. These are called
the Pacific Rim countries, as many of
them lie around the edge of the Pacific
ocean. Two-thirds of Australia's trade is

LARGEST IMPORTS IN 1991–92 ($A million)

2,556	road vehicles
2,168	aircraft and associated equipment
1,924	office and automatic data processing machines
1,577	petrol and oils

LARGEST EXPORTS IN 1991–92 ($A million)

coal	6,848
gold	4,023
iron ore concentrates	2,850
meat of bovine animals	2,777

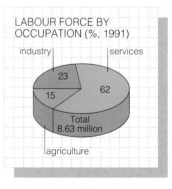
LABOUR FORCE BY OCCUPATION (%, 1991)
industry 23, 15, services 62, Total 8.63 million, agriculture

◀ *Gladstone Power Station in Queensland is a major supplier of electricity to both domestic and industrial consumers.*

▲ Surfers Paradise, Queensland, is one of the most popular resorts both for Australians and for foreign tourists. Numerous high-rise hotels fringe the long beach here.

now with Pacific Rim countries. Britain was once Australia's main trading partner, but this changed when the UK joined the European Community. Its place has been taken by Japan, with the USA a close second, followed by New Zealand, South Korea and Singapore. Nearly a quarter of all goods entering Australia from abroad come from the USA, followed by Japan at 19% and Britain at 6%.

One of the major concerns for trade abroad centres on barriers or rules made by other countries which work against free trade for Australian companies. Trade barriers make exporting difficult, because the goods become too expensive for people to buy. The Australian government has been working hard to overcome these obstacles. For instance, agreements have been signed that secure closer economic ties with New Zealand, to eliminate trade barriers and to promote the exchange of goods between the two countries.

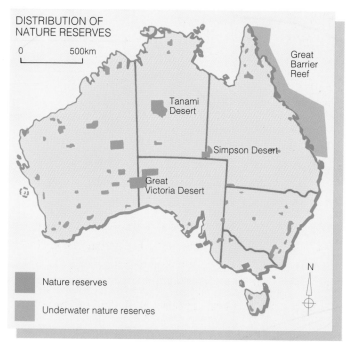

DISTRIBUTION OF
NATURE RESERVES

0   500km

Great
Barrier
Reef

Tanami
Desert

Simpson Desert

Great
Victoria Desert

N

Nature reserves

Underwater nature reserves

parts of the country this has resulted in
desertification. The other main soil problem
is the build-up of natural salts, due to the
excessive use of irrigation water.

Another major environmental hazard is
bush fires, the most serious natural hazard
in Australia in terms of loss of life over the
last 50 years. Devastating examples
occurred around Sydney between 7 and 12
January 1994. By the time the fires had
been brought under control, four people
had been killed and over 200 homes

▶ *Kangaroos are some of the best
known of Australia's wild animals. They
are a form of marsupial, the name given
to animals which carry their young in
a pouch.*

▶ *The salt-water crocodile inhabits the* MANGROVE *swamps and marshes of Australia's tropical coastline. This one was photographed in Western Australia.*

destroyed. The total damage was estimated at $A 150 million.

On the positive side, Australia has one of the largest collections of pollution-free, solar-energy generating facilities in the world. It also has some of the most extensive areas of untouched natural beauty on Earth, with many unique species of plants and animals.

▶ *A koala with a baby on her back. Koalas, which feed only on eucalyptus leaves, are one of the traditional symbols of Australia.*

▼ *The Pinnacles Desert, in Western Australia, has been sculpted by the erosion of weak sandstone rocks.*

KEY FACTS

● Australia has some of the world's biggest deserts, including the Simpson, Gibson and Great Sandy.
● Approximately 43.2 million hectares of pastoral land are affected by erosion.
● There are 6 World Heritage Sites in Australia, so called because of their outstanding natural beauty and scientific importance.
● About 90% of the state of New South Wales has problems with soil erosion.

▚ THE FUTURE

What will the future hold for Australia? Already more people are moving to the big cities and so many smaller outback towns are declining. The population will increase as the birth rate rises. At the same time, people will live longer, putting pressure on crowded residential and work places.

Australia is also likely to cut its last formal tie to Britain. By the year 2001, the centenary of independence, the country may be a republic with a President as head of state rather than Queen Elizabeth II.

Many farms are inefficient and are being updated. Others will close because of low

▼ *The skyline of Perth in Western Australia, one of the cities that is drawing people to move from rural to urban areas.*

▲*Queen Elizabeth II, seen here in Western Australia, is head of state. There are suggestions that she may be replaced by a President.*

KEY FACTS

● By 2001 there will be 3 million people over 60 years old, compared with 2 million in 1981.

● Some studies predict that in 2030 Australian temperatures will be between 0.3° and 2.5°C higher than their 1990 levels.

● Satellite links are being updated to improve communications, particularly for children who are members of the School of the Air.

▼ *Australia's future lies with its people, a young population of many nationalities living in a country rich in natural resources and potential.*

productivity of over-used land. There is a move to conserve the environment more in areas where agriculture is a big money-maker. The future is likely to see an increase in both manufacturing industry and mining activities.

Important changes are taking place to support the Aborigines. In the past they had poor access to housing, hospitals and schools, for example. This is an increasingly important issue, and recent legislation, known as Mabo, gives Aborigines new rights over places such as Uluru.

The young people of today are regarded as Australia's hope for the future. With careful planning, the country can look forward to a prosperous 21st century as one of the key nations in the southern hemisphere.

FURTHER INFORMATION

● AUSTRALIAN HIGH COMMISSION
Australia House, Strand, London WC2B 4LA
Has a library and leaflets on Australia, and
provides general information.

● AUSTRALIAN STUDIES CENTRE
27 Russell Square, London WC1B 5DS
Has a library and leaflets on Australia.

● AUSTRALIAN TOURIST COMMISSION
10 Putney Hill, London SW15 6AA
Provides a range of tourist information
on Australia.

● AUSTRALIAN FILM COMMISSION
Victory House, 99 Regent Street,
London W1R 6HB
Has leaflets and audio-visual material
on Australia.

BOOKS ABOUT AUSTRALIA

Australia, Andrew Kelly, Wayland 1991
(age 9–12)
Focus on Australia, Heather Foote,
Evans 1991 (age 9–12)
Australia, Ian James, Franklin Watts 1989
(age 9–12)

GLOSSARY

BILLABONG

A small water spring.

CAPITALISM

An economic system in which individuals
own businesses and keep the profits.

CYCLONE

A violent storm which usually brings strong
winds and torrential rain.

DESERTIFICATION

The deterioration of land into desert
conditions, due to factors such as lack
of rain, lack of trees and soil erosion.

DIDJERIDU

An Aboriginal musical instrument,
consisting of a long, hollow, wooden tube
that produces a low-pitched sound.

GROUND WATER

Water which is found beneath the surface
of the Earth.

IRRIGATION

The spreading of water across the ground
surface, usually to allow the growing of
crops.

MANGROVE

A type of vegetation that is typical of
tropical swamp lands.

OUTBACK

Remote parts of Australia.

PAVLOVA

A type of dessert based on meringue and
cream, often with kiwi fruit.

ROAD TRAIN

A large, articulated lorry with many trailers,
used to transport goods by road.

SALINIZATION

The build-up of natural salts in the soil,
frequently due to irrigation, which makes
the soil infertile.

INDEX

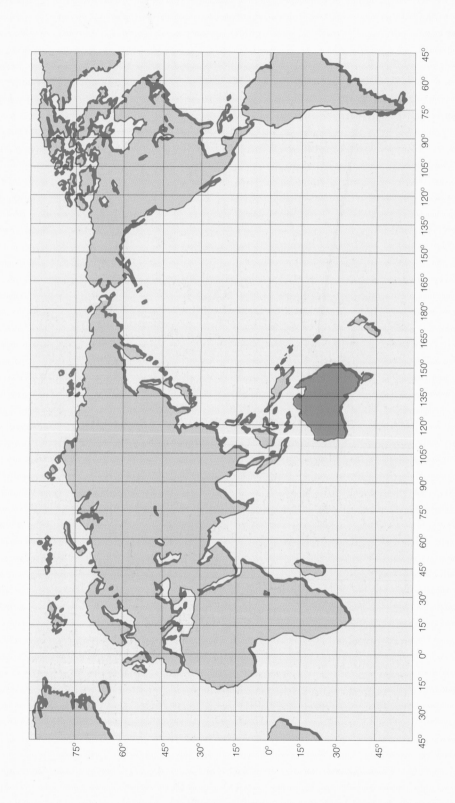

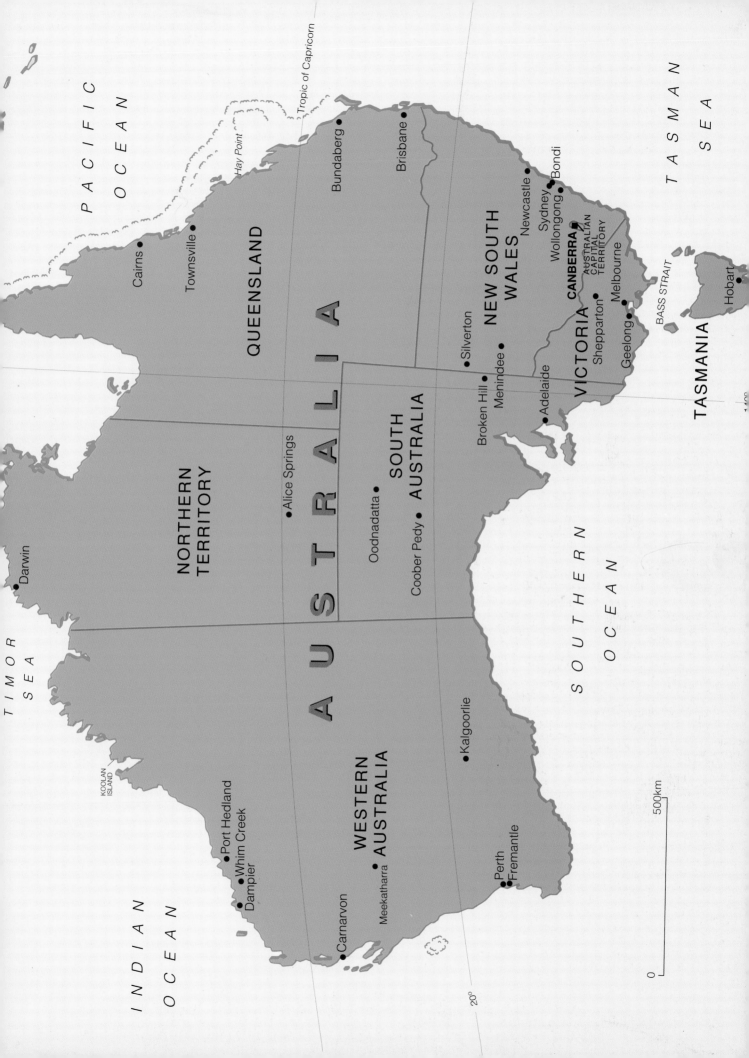